Into *the* FOREGROUND

A Century of Scottish Women in Photographs

Leah Leneman

Photographs selected by
Alison Cromarty and
Susan Irvine

Captions by
Jenni Calder

NATIONAL MUSEUMS OF SCOTLAND

ALAN SUTTON PUBLISHING

National Museums of Scotland
Chambers Street, Edinburgh EH1 1JF

Alan Sutton Publishing
Phoenix Mill, Far Thrupp, Stroud, Gloucestershire

Alan Sutton Publishing Inc
83 Washington Street, Dover NH 03820, USA

First published 1993
Copyright © Text Leah Leneman 1993
Copyright © Captions Trustees of the National Museums of
Scotland 1993

ISBN 0 7509 0444 5 (hardback)
    0 7509 0539 5 (paperback)

British Library Cataloguing-in-Publication Data
A catalogue record for this book is available from the British
Library

Front cover: Gutting herring, Nairn, 1920s
Back cover: Bondagers at Cornhill-on-Tweed, 1908-9

Designed by the Publications Office of the
National Museums of Scotland in association with
David Frame Creative Services, Edinburgh
Filmset in Monotype Bembo by David Frame Creative, Edinburgh
Printed and bound in Great Britain by
The Bath Press, Avon

CONTENTS

'Robert Davidson and second daughter' reads the original caption to this 1887 photograph of the blacksmith at Stobs Woodfoot, Roxburghshire. The accompanying information mentions two sons, Walter and John, but neither wife nor daughters feature. The nameless daughter has no identity, except through her father. He is in his working clothes, while she is dressed up.

PREFACE

I am tempted to paraphrase Virginia Woolf and say, as a Scotswoman I have no history: an exaggeration but not untrue. The past twenty years have seen a remarkable increase in work in women's history: reclamation and discovery, rewriting our understanding of the past; and asking *why* women's work and concerns should so readily be buried and forgotten. But little of that work has focused on Scotland.

For example, I was a student when I discovered the suffragettes (school history did not concern itself with such a marginal issue) and read everything I could get my hands on about them. It was years later that I found out that there had been a major Scottish campaign and that they had (probably) burnt down my local station.

Then again, I seem to know very little about the rest of Scottish history – beyond stories about watching spiders and the like. Though I know – well, knew – rather a lot about Napoleon and Lord Shaftesbury. Again there has been a growth in work on Scottish history of recent years, but in it women's voices are not often heard.

It is an absence we fill with misperceptions and with stereotypes. Overshadowed by both the stories of the English and the stories of men, Scottish women have been doubly hidden from history. But now that is changing, thanks to the work of a small band of historians and writers, and it is as a vivid and accessible contribution to a growing movement of rediscovery that I particularly welcome this book.

I welcome it because it gives the lie to still-accepted clichés: a woman's place was never only in the home. But because women also have a domestic role, not least among the book's pleasures is the insight it gives into their homes. I welcome it because of the quality of the photographs and their extraordinary variety: women in their Sunday best and women in tatters, women with children, women on outings together, women political activists, the women medical graduates (such a brave few of them), the Women's Timber Corps. Often, the contrasts are striking, and thought-provoking. I want to know all their stories. Only a few images feel already familiar: a bride, a Shetland woman knitting.

Because ideas of what women *should* be like, and manufactured images of women, have played such a big part in forming our perceptions, this more direct, less mediated information on some women's live is especially important. It shows that our world has never accorded with competing stereotypes, but is created by complex, contradictory, living women and girls, men and boys.

I welcome too the brief windows opened on 'ordinary' life, with its washing to be done and hens to be fed, tatties to be peeled (some things change more than others). I welcome the evocative images of 'ordinary' fun: four young women on a picnic, an incongruously elegant group of friends paddling, their wide hats tied with muslin scarves. It is perhaps my favourite, though it vies with the bondagers in the fields – tulip fields in Scotland, imagine! – and the truly extraordinary galleon hairstyle.

But I also welcome this collection simply for itself, as an enjoyable selection of well-chosen and sometimes beautiful pictures; one I can look at with my daughters and say, look, that was the work your great-granny did, and look, I remember when granma had a hat like that!

Sue Innes

INTRODUCTION

Why a book of photographs of Scottish *women* over the past century? Women are not a minority, nor a curiosity, but part of the fabric of life in Scotland, as everywhere else. So why single them out in this way?

An answer lies in the symbols of Scottish identity: whisky, the kilt, the bagpipes – all very masculine. And what about the names that spring to mind? Robert the Bruce, Bonnie Prince Charlie, Robbie Burns, Sir Walter Scott – apart from the archetypal victim, Mary, Queen of Scots, they are all male. It is partly to correct such a distorted view of Scotland's past that women's presence needs representation.

Another answer is that women have always been so much a part of the fabric of life, so much of the time in the background of men's lives, that they were hardly seen. Fortunately, the keen eyes of photographers have captured the strength, the humour, the joy and sorrow on women's faces and in their actions. To reproduce such photographs in a book is not merely to look with the eyes of the present at women in the past but in some cases to see them as they were rarely seen – because hardly noticed – at the time.

Inevitably, the photographic record is also a distortion. Particularly in the early days of photography, pictures were taken of the unusual, the exceptional, the valued, while women's lives were largely composed of the ordinary, the humdrum, the unvalued. It is ironic that we owe some pictures of women – particularly in the Highlands and Islands – to the fact that the humdrum and ordinary in one culture can seem extraordinary to the eyes of an outsider. Gathering together pictures from the Scottish Ethnological Archive for this collection has been revealing because, as the subject categories do not reflect women's activities, no one knew what the Archive actually contained in the way of such photographs of women until the whole collection had been gone through.

But is there something so distinctive about *Scottish* women that they need singling out? Although part of Great Britain, Scotland still has, as it always did have, characteristics and a culture quite separate from her southern neighbours. This book, in line with others in the series, celebrates that culture. And, by celebrating it through the unfamiliar medium of Scottish women, a new perspective is gained.

There is a popular idea with regard to women in Scotland that progress has been continuous – that way back in time they were really badly off, and since then things have gradually got better and better until our comparatively enlightened era was reached. Nothing could be further from the truth: a cyclical rather than a linear progression is much closer to reality.

Before the invention of photography, our knowledge of the past was based on the written record, augmented by paintings. Here we get more distortion, because the written record was largely concerned with the exercise of power, and that power was in the hands of men. But, as with the successful search through the Ethnological Archive subject categories for pictures for women, so a search through written records created for entirely different purposes can reveal aspects of women's lives. Before looking at the century of photographs, it is therefore useful to have some idea of what those lives were like in earlier centuries.

Not surprisingly, the further back in time one goes the harder it is to find out about women's lives. However, we do know a little about women in Celtic society in the seventh and eighth centuries. At that time, both marriage partners had equal status in the marriage contract, and the marriage could be dissolved by common consent. Women had more real power than in many later centuries.

In medieval Scotland princesses, queens, aristocrats, and abbesses found their way into the written records and because of those records we know that some of them wielded immense power, usually behind the scenes. In Highland society there were women poets – *The Book of the Dean of Lismore*, compiled between 1512 and 1526, contains examples. It is a myth that in this social class women always accepted the marriage arrangements made by their parents, for medieval Scottish court books have cases in them of refusals by women to marry the man chosen by parents (and there could be no marriage without the consent of the woman). Nor was marriage necessarily for life in pre-Reformation Scotland, for amongst the aristocracy at least, marriages were dissolved and second partners taken with surprising ease.

There are records for this period of women in Scottish burghs, revealing that some of humble status earned their living not only as servants and wet nurses but also in skilled trades as seamstresses, and bonnet-makers, and in other crafts. There were female shopkeepers and merchants in Edinburgh and other towns. These trades were strictly controlled, and entry to them depended on the agreement of the existing burgesses, yet women in the pre-Reformation period were admitted as burgesses. Most of them were widows who took over their husband's businesses, but not all, and there were no objections to women working outside the home in this way.

Fashions in clothing changed at various times in the course of these centuries, but it was only the women of the gentry who could afford to follow fashion's decrees. For the mass of women clothing simply had to be practical and hard-wearing.

After the 1560s, the Reformation brought changes. With the new stress on education and with schools being set up in every parish, there should have been more opportunities for girls, but in practice schooling for the humbler classes was still largely confined to boys. Church courts were set up across the country, regulating everyday life, with public appearances in front of the congregation required to purge a sin. As the most obvious evidence of sin was pregnancy in an unmarried woman, many women had to undergo public humiliation. However, if a woman expressed repentance and made her public appearances, then the slate was wiped clean. If she later wanted to move to another parish she would be given a certificate attesting to her good name.

This was the period in which a horrifyingly large number of women were executed for witchcraft in Scotland. In a society of tightly bound communities where every move was watched, deviations from the norm could result in a charge of sorcery, and proving innocence of something so vague but so generally believed was almost impossible. On the other hand, 'witch' featured among the nasty names like 'whore' that a woman might be called, without anyone assuming that it was a genuine accusation. (A woman thus slandered could turn to the parish church court for redress without fear of sparking, literally, a witchhunt.) In the late seventeenth century, women were prominent among the Covenanters who defied the government and the Established Church in the southwest of the country.

Going into domestic service was usual for girls (and also for many boys), but this did not mean the formality of later decades; quite humble households would have serving lasses and lads, who might well come from a family of similar standing in the same parish. A girl could legally marry at twelve but, apart from the wealthy aristocratic families where marriages were arranged for economic or dynastic reasons, most women did not marry until their mid-twenties because a married couple was expected to have enough money to set up an independent household.

Cooking, washing and spinning were traditional parts of a woman's work, and in the towns women could earn a living offering those services to others, particularly to aristocratic and gentry households who came to Edinburgh for a short season. Widows and other women continued to run businesses, particularly selling clothing and cloth, and food. There were plenty of female taverners, brewers and tapsters, and the fishwife was a familiar figure in Scottish towns from an early date. In the late seventeenth century, when post offices were first set up, there were some women postmasters, and in the 1690s the King's printer was a woman and Edinburgh had a woman bookseller. In other words, before 1700 women had far more varied job opportunities than they would later. At that time most of the servants in big houses were men. Educational opportunities for women were expanding though still mainly confined to the gentry. Reading was encouraged because it gave access to the Bible, but writing was not considered necessary.

On the land certain tasks were considered women's province. Women looked after the cows and did most dairy work. In the Highlands transhumance – moving the cattle to the summer shielings – gave women a particularly important role since all the daily work of herding and attention to milk cows was their responsibility.

In some ways the eighteenth century was a particularly good one for women in Scotland. The church still held its grip on rural parishes, and women who had borne illegitimate children but performed their public penance were still able to get certificates attesting to their good character, but the humanising breath of the Enlightenment meant a far less rigorous chastisement of sinners. Men and women servants were free to work together unsupervised in a way that would be inconceivable a century later.

In towns a woman could now be found as a teacher, brewer, midwife, trader, bonnetmaker, postmistress, shopkeeper, alehouse keeper, and lodging-house keeper. There were also 'naughty' women in bawdy houses, which the Church tried – unsuccessfully – to drive out. Though women's participation in trade was mostly confined to shopkeeping, their names could be found amongst international merchants. Rural women made a substantial contribution to the family income: in the mid-eighteenth century approximately 80% of adult women in Scotland were involved in spinning, many producing yarn for sale.

On the negative side, in the early eighteenth century females were still employed in ways that would horrify later generations. In south-east Scotland wives and daughters of coal miners acted as bearers. In some pits they outnumbered men two to one. Bearers carried loads of up to 75 kilos along low passages and up stepladders to the pit head, some twenty times a day.

Although the consent of parents to a marriage was not a legal requirement in Scotland, couples nevertheless had parental pressure to deal with; the rise in irregular marriages in the eighteenth century thus gave women greater freedom. Couples no longer had to have the banns called nor be married by their minister, and there were well-known irregular marriers in Edinburgh to whom they could resort. This did mean that some men married bigamously, but the freedom to choose who, when and where to marry with no outside interference led to a positive fashion for irregular marrying. Whether married regularly or irregularly, until the mid-nineteenth century Scottish women kept their own surnames.

By the early nineteenth century some new occupations were listed amongst the more traditional. *The Edinburgh Post Office Directory* of 1824-5 included many women dressmakers and quite a few milliners. Some 344 women offered lodgings, though this, of course, was something they had done for centuries past. Midwifery was another respected female occupation in the eighteenth and early nineteenth centuries, and formal training for it existed. Women writers now began to make an impact. Anne Grant of Laggan was one of the most influential figures in creating a romanticized image of the Highlands in Lowland Scotland, and Lady Nairn's Jacobite songs became the mainstay of romantic Jacobitism throughout the century.

The political agitations of the first half of the nineteenth century, such as Chartism, involved women but only in support of their menfolk. When so few men had the vote, it was not yet time for women to demand that right, but after the 1834 Reform Act, and with growing literacy and political involvement among middle-class women, it was a different story. A Scotswoman, Marion Reid, produced a powerful argument for females to be granted the parliamentary franchise in *A Plea for Women*, published in 1843.

By this time the gulf between the classes had widened. With more and more goods being produced in factories, it became a point of pride among middle-class men that their wives and daughters did not have to lift a finger, and as time went on such women were increasingly restricted to a narrow life of leisure. With new standards of cleanliness for all except the unrespectable poor, the weekly wash (lasting from Monday to Wednesday) became a great burden in most households. This also meant a more pressing need for domestic servants, and in 1851 more than 10% of the total female population in Scotland were classified as such.

After the elaborate clothing of the eighteenth century, the fashion at the beginning of the nineteenth was for simple, high-waisted gowns and no corsetry or padding. However, by the time Queen Victoria came to the throne women's clothing was again becoming constricting. As the role of middle and upper-class women was increasingly seen as mainly a decorative one, so the constrictions and impracticalities of stays and petticoats – and eventually, the bustle – became the norm for such women.

Before industrialization women worked within the family economy, particularly at spinning. But during the early years of industrialization they were drawn into factories: of 59,314 workers in Scottish textiles in 1839, 40,868 (69%) were female, though nearly half of them were under eighteen. In a city such as Dundee, where the majority of the workforce was female, there was plenty of camaraderie, though even here there was a gulf between weavers, who were the 'respectable' workers, and the spinners, who were the boisterous, rowdier ones. In 1841, domestic service, agriculture, clothing and textiles employed about 90% of the female labour workforce.

Changes in farming, and the growth of heavy industry which required adult male labour, led to the increasing use of female labour on the land from the 1830s onwards. Women were known to be better at certain tasks, like hand-weeding and gathering at the grain harvest. More to the point, the employer only had to pay them half a man's wage. In 1851, there were 26,150 females in Scotland classified as agricultural workers, but this is likely to be a low estimate since so much of the work was seasonal, part-time or casual.

The acceptance of female sexuality that characterized the previous century was replaced by a narrow, rigid outlook, whereby 'respectability' was all-important, and a woman seeking domestic service would have to produce a reference of impeccable character in order to have a hope of a post. In rural areas women who worked on the land, and those who followed the fishing fleets and worked as gutters, had a hard life but a freer one than the increasing numbers who went into domestic service.

The behaviour of Scottish people – at least among the working classes – did not always conform to the Victorian ideal, for Scotland had a high proportion of illegitimate births compared with the British average, and bridal pregnancies too were common, though this varied a great deal between different parts of Scotland. More children lived, family size grew, and many women were tied to constant childbearing.

In the Highlands and Islands women were at the forefront of some of the battles that ensued when landowners began to replace people with sheep. In the subsistence existence of crofting their skills and their contributions proved crucial. During the fishing season, in areas such as Shetland where men left their crofts for months at a time, it was the women who did all the work on the land. But they made their own entertainment, with ceilidhs and other community efforts.

In 1867, when a second Reform Act gave many more men the vote but included no women, agitation began for the franchise, and the Edinburgh National Society for Women's Suffrage formed branches in many parts of Scotland. One woman in particular, Jane Taylour from Stranraer, travelled all over the country, as far north as Orkney and Shetland, to speak on the subject. By this time, women with a good secondary education were demanding to be allowed entry to university. Organizations were formed in Edinburgh and Glasgow to agitate for women's higher education, and for other issues relating to women's rights. Because medicine had become professionalized it was a masculine preserve. With Sophia Jex-Blake's fight to gain medical training, Edinburgh became the centre of this controversy. The second half of the nineteenth century was a period of polarization between the sexes, but at the same time one in which educational opportunities expanded and women started to fight for change.

Before the time of photography, therefore, there were centuries of change in Scotland, with periods when women had comparative freedom and others when they were more restricted and controlled. Just before the photographs begin, the heavy blanket of 'respectability' that smothered Victorian Scotland was beginning to lift and a breath of fresh air was blowing through the country.

To sum up and encompass the lives of women as diverse as crofters, domestic servants, factory workers, aristocrats, middle-class women of leisure who were happy to be so, others who devoted themselves to charitable efforts, and still others who demanded a university education and a profession, is impossible. The photographs speak for themselves; the words simply put them into context.

Scottish Ethnological Archive

All the photographs in this book are from the Scottish Ethnological Archive in the National Museums of Scotland except those on p 48 and p 49 which come from the National Library of Scotland and are reproduced here with kind permission of the Trustees. Most of the Archive's photographs have been either donated to or purchased by the Archive, or lent for copying by individual owners. A few were copied from the photographic collections of other institutions.

The Archive's aims are to record and preserve documentary and illustrative material as context to the social history collections of the National Museums, and to provide a research tool for museum staff and public alike. The collection consists of photographs, slides, postcards and film; drawings and maps; audio tapes; manuscript sources such as diaries and account books; newspaper cuttings, bibliographies and notes extracted from documentary and printed sources.

In the photographs included here, the photographers are always named where they are known, and all known individuals are named. Should any readers be able to identify unnamed people or places, or wish to contribute to the Archive's collection, Dorothy Kidd, curator of the Archive, would be very pleased to hear from them.

Woman with a basket of goose-
berries, sitting outside a house in
Campbeltown, Argyllshire, about
1900.

THE VICTORIAN WOMAN

The closing decades of the nineteenth century saw many changes for women in Scotland. The Victorian ideal of the middle-class woman as purely decorative had led to a stereotype of women as creatures controlled by their emotions and inferior to men, but by the 1890s fresh images were emerging. The 'new woman', who sought emancipation from traditional restraints, became a recognized heroine (or bogey figure, depending on one's standpoint). The new medium of photography began to reflect this changing imagery, to mirror male fantasies of women as well as recording reality.

Women could at last obtain university degrees – the first eight women were admitted to a Scottish university, Edinburgh, in 1892, and they could qualify as doctors too. Although they could not yet vote for their MPs, they could now vote in local elections and join political organizations such as Scottish Women's Liberal Associations or, for Conservatives, the Primrose League.

But it was not just the high flyers who spanned new horizons, for there was a great broadening of opportunities, and it no longer put a woman beyond the pale to earn her own living. The teaching and nursing professions offered secure, 'respectable' employment, and since from the time it was invented the typewriter had – for no obvious reason – been associated with women, female clerks were now displacing males (though most secretaries were still men).

With so many new openings in towns, women began to leave the land. According to the 1871 census 26% of those employed in agriculture were female, against a mere 6% in England. The census did not include the seasonal labourers who sowed, harvested and gathered crops. Yet it counted 22,174 Scottish women as agricultural labourers. By the 1890s farmers throughout Lowland Scotland were complaining of a shortage of women workers, blamed mainly on rising expectations. However, the perception of hordes of women leaving the land is not borne out by the 1891 census which classified 22,046 Scottish women as agricultural labourers.

An alternative to farm work was domestic service, seen as more 'genteel', though certainly no easier. In 1873 it was calculated that a housemaid worked from 6am to 10pm, with 2½ hours for meals and 1½ hours for 'needlework' in the afternoon. This totalled 12 hours, which was 2 hours more than factory women worked. Throughout the late Victorian period about 9% of the total female population were domestic servants – the largest female occupational group.

Women in the north increasingly joined the seasonal migrations of the fishing crews in the supporting roles on shore of cleaning, gutting, salting and packing fish.

Because they were seen as unusual and picturesque, the camera often recorded them. Hard and unpleasant the work might have been, but they enjoyed camaraderie and the freedom to behave as boisterously as they wished without the censorious eye of a superior on them.

Middle-class women increasingly took part in sports – golf, tennis, hockey, swimming. Even more important in the emancipation of women at this time was the growth of cycling as a 'respectable' activity (for adults). By 1896 about a third of orders for bicycles in Britain were from women, and that activity offered unprecedented freedom and equality between the sexes. Related to this was a call for more rational clothing for women, though the norm was still corseted and movement-restricting.

Joanna Kerr, Mrs John Dickie, photographed around the late 1850s or '60s. Her full-skirted silk dress is characteristic of the late 1850s. Underneath it she probably wore a hoop, and the white collar and false sleeves could be removed for washing. At this time women wore indoor caps. Mrs Dickie's is of black lace and velvet. The books beside her suggest a woman of serious purpose.
J Gilchrist, Edinburgh

Mrs Beaumont and her great grand-children, Helen and George Newton, in Dundee around 1860. Mrs Beaumont, in her black wool dress and black lace cap, is probably a widow. Just visible under Helen's silk dress is the broderie anglaise edging of her pantalettes. Her hair was wrapped in rags overnight to produce her ringlets. George, like all small boys at the time, also wears a dress.
J Abbot, Dundee

Gayfield Square School for Girls,
Edinburgh, 1865. The school, at
2 Gayfield Square, a site now
occupied by a police station, was
for blind girls. It was closed about
1877-8, when the West Craigmillar
Asylum for the Blind was
completed.

Trainee teachers at a college at Crail, Fife, in 1875-6. With the Education Act, which made education compulsory for all children from five to thirteen, the demand for certificated teachers grew. The clothes and hair styles – which include a number of what look like false hair pieces – of these young women suggest they dressed especially for the photographer.

Caught in action walking down a street in Fortrose, Ross-shire, probably late nineteenth century. Hats and glove were *de rigueur* for out-of-doors. The woman in the centre is carrying an umbrella.

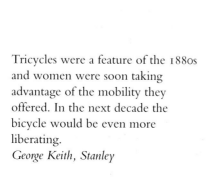

Tricycles were a feature of the 1880s and women were soon taking advantage of the mobility they offered. In the next decade the bicycle would be even more liberating.
George Keith, Stanley

Cyclists at Bridge of Cally, Perthshire, probably 1899. They look as if they are about to receive a good send-off. The woman seated in the centre is Mrs Helen Butchart, with her daughter-in-law Mary (born 1843) behind her. The woman and girl with bicycles are Ada Butchart (born about 1870) and Kathleen Burns (born 1885).

Elizabeth Haldane of Cloan, Perthshire, described the bicycle as 'the liberator of womanhood'. She went on:

'A woman had to take her courage in her hands to mount even a safety bicycle, for it betokened something fast, and our full skirts and petticoats were not well adapted for the work. Mercifully coats and skirts came into vogue before long, perhaps incited to do so by the new form of locomotion, and along with them came sailor hats; and hence the lady cyclist in the end presented quite a good and tidy appearance, though various means had to be adopted of so fastening her skirts on her legs as to prevent them entangling themselves in the back wheel, or worse still showing her legs to the public, an unforgiveable offence... '
(*From One Century to Another*, London 1937)

Towering women, photographed at Mount Esk, Lasswade, Midlothian, in 1884. The third and fourth from the top are Janet and Christian Steuart.

In 1853 James Steuart, Writer to the Signet and grandfather of Janet and Christian, bought Mount Esk to use as a summer residence. The family continued to divide their time between Edinburgh and Lasswade until 1939. Janet and Christian were two of a family of seven, several of whom – including the two girls – took photographs.

The Steuart girls, Janet and Christian, eight years later, again photographed at Mount Esk but this time in more formal dress and pose.

Spinning on a treadle-operated horizontal flax wheel in the 1890s, in a house near Insch, Aberdeenshire. Spinning remained a common activity in many rural homes, often pursued in the evenings when the other household tasks were done.

Flax spinning wheels were similar to those used for wool, but incorporated a distaff for holding the prepared fibres, and frequently had a recess for a water pot. The spinner kept her fingers moist with the water, which allowed her to spin a smoother yarn.

Kitchen maid peeling potatoes at
Old Kirk Manse, Corstorphine,
Edinburgh, 1880s. Even households
of quite modest size were dependent
on domestic service for cleaning and
cooking.

Young women feeding the poultry,
possibly in Midlothian, early 1900s.
This is clearly a posed photograph,
perhaps of the mistress of the house
(centre) and two servants. All three
look self-conscious. None of them
appear to be taking the activity
seriously – indeed, the empty beer
bottles at the door emphasise the
possibility that the photograph was
taken as a joke.

Milking in the 1890s. The women
are wearing the striped aprons
typical of dairymaids on the larger
farms of central and south-west
Scotland. This is also a posed
photograph, but milking out-of-
doors was common.

Baiting fishing lines, Newhaven, 1890s. The woman in the centre is shelling bait, probably mussels, while the others attach the bait to the lines. The lines were then carefully laid into the skulls – wooden containers – from which they were cast once on the boats at sea. On the left, nets are hung over a boat to dry.

Although women did not go to sea, they were heavily involved in the fishing industry, providing an essential support. As well as helping with preparations for fishing, they often processed the fish and sold the catch.
J Patrick

Market in the Castlegate, Aberdeen, about 1900. At the turn of the century much daily shopping for provisions was still carried out at the weekly Friday market. The stall on the right is probably selling second-hand clothes; the poor rarely bought their clothes new. The girl in the foreground is bare-footed, while the young woman beyond her carries a small child wrapped in a plaid.

The drawing room of Larchgrove House, Balerno, Midlothian, around 1900. Throughout the Victorian period the home was pre-eminently the sphere of women, whose role it was to maintain it as a place of comfort, security and domestic virtue.

Washday at the Sligachan Hotel, Skye. This photograph was taken between 1873 and 1884, during the time when John Alexander Butters was proprietor. The hotel servants are treading the blankets in wooden tubs with their bare feet, with the woman on the right using a stick to ring out the washing. The water has been drawn from the river.
George Washington Wilson

A group of women enjoying a picnic, possibly near Greenock, Renfrewshire, about 1900. By this time middle-class women were more likely to spend time outdoors, and not necessarily in the company of men. There was an increasing enthusiasm for the benefits of fresh air and exercise.

With hats firmly anchored against the breeze and long skirts raised, these women paddle on the beach at Campbeltown, Argyll, about 1900. By the end of the nineteenth century the seaside holiday was becoming popular – and more accessible, with improvements in transport and the provision of paid holidays.
McGrory Collection, Campbeltown Library

Housemaid at work, 1903. Helen Mathieson at 19 Correnie Gardens, Edinburgh. The effort to keep carpets clean before the widespread use of vacuum cleaners was considerable. In large households, several housemaids would have been employed. There were three at 19 Correnie Gardens, the home of William Graham, banker and author of *The One Pound Note*.
Dr C W Graham

THE EDWARDIAN WOMAN

The pace of change quickened after the turn of the century. Some middle-class ladies of means still led lives of leisure, but they were atypical. They may have had no need to earn a living, but there were many charitable activities to fill their hours. And if they did want to live independent lives they could get a post as a nurse or a teacher or a clerk – though they would get paid only about half a man's salary.

Whereas in 1851 roughly 35% of teachers were women, by 1911 women teachers accounted for 70%. But they could not rise higher than infant mistress in an elementary school, for men still dominated the higher levels of the profession. While there were five times as many male clerks in 1911 than there had been in 1868, there were 400 times as many women clerks. But cameras did not penetrate into offices, so there are no photographs of them. Indoor shots were difficult to take, but they exist of women factory workers, albeit not represented in this collection, so the lack clearly has more to do with the humdrum nature of office work. Works outings, as 'occasions', were a different matter.

With all the new opportunities in the towns, women now really were deserting the land: compared to the 22,000 Scottish female agricultural workers in 1891, in 1911 there were only about 6000. But this figure did not include seasonal workers, nor the wives and daughters of farmers, crofters and smallholders, who worked every bit as hard as their menfolk.

Fisher girls who did the gutting and packing worked from 6am to 6pm three nights a week, 6am to 9pm the other three nights, and until midnight on Saturday to finish the herring – often in cold, wet conditions. But however exhausting the life, they were part of a strongly-knit crowd of young people, leaving home each year for different places.

When it came to the professions, women were still struggling to gain a foothold. They could now qualify as doctors, though many hospitals would not employ them, so they accepted less prestigious posts in mental institutions or in public health, or went abroad as medical missionaries. A woman could not practise at all as a lawyer or be employed in many other professions. And – most galling of all – she still could not vote for her candidate for Parliament.

The suffrage movement is the best remembered part of Edwardian women's history, and rightly so, for it united women the length and breadth of the country, from Dumfries to Shetland. Most supporters of the movement were non-militant.

Ann Watt shelling mussels for bait in her home at Gardenstown, Banffshire, 1906. The home was often the setting of a woman's work, whether or not the environment was suited to the task.

Ann Forbes, born 1851, was the daughter of Christian Sim and George Forbes, fisherman. She married Gilbert Watt in 1872 at Gamrie (Gardenstown). They had five daughters and three sons. Above her head is Gilbert Watt's membership certificate of the local freemasons' lodge.

A bride photographed in the early 1900s. We don't know who she is, though the photograph may have been taken in Edinburgh. She clearly comes from a comfortably-off background. The fans on the wall suggest the oriental influence which was fashionable towards the end of the nineteenth century.

The late nineteenth century saw a ripple of rebellion against traditional marriage, but it remained an aspiration for most women.

Mrs Jenkins and baby daughter Jean beside the Water of Leith between Stockbridge and Canonmills, Edinburgh, about 1902. Mrs Jenkins looks as if she is dressed for a special occasion – perhaps Jean's christening? This photograph was taken by her husband George.

Kirstie MacDonald, photographed in Ross Street, Tain, Ross-shire, in 1910. She was probably one of a group of travelling people, or tinkers as they would then have been called. Tinkers were itinerant traders who dealt in goods such as metal wares, brushes and baskets. Some were descendants of dispossessed Highland peasantry, others of gypsies.

Kirstie MacDonald earned 2d a drill hoeing turnips. It was said that, certified dead by a local doctor, a nurse and a neighbour prepared to wash her body. As they tried to take off what they thought were black woollen stockings she sat up saying, 'Och, och, that's sair' – she had no stockings on.
Donald Macleod

Lying-in ward at Greenlea Hospital, Edinburgh, 1904-14. This was a poorhouse and the women were homeless. Although to late twentieth-century eyes this interior has a rather forbidding austerity, it offered standards of care and cleanliness which were impossible in many homes. Many women with accommodation of their own had their babies in squalid circumstances and without medical attention.

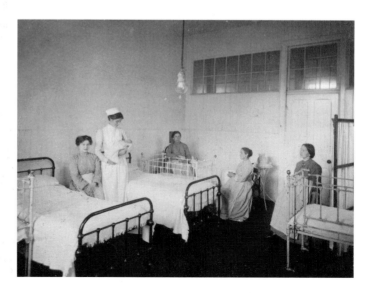

An advertisement for hen feed – Flock Took and Took Took. These were products of the firm of Macfarlan, Shearer and Co, agricultural merchants in Greenock, Renfrewshire. The use of images of attractive, smiling women to encourage the customer is almost as old as advertising itself.

Catherine MacLaren (Mrs Angus MacDonald) feeding the hens at Morar, Inverness-shire, about 1905. She is holding something in her right hand – perhaps a chick? The thatched hut is the hen house.
M E M Donaldson

'In some Highland districts hens were considered unclean creatures; in others they were regarded almost as pets. This *cailleach* (old woman) calls "Pic, pic" for the hens to come and be fed outside her ramshackle, thatched shanty. An old boat, turned upside down, was often used as a hen house.'
(John Telfer-Dunbar, *M E M Donaldson, Herself*)

Sir John Gilmour Bt and Mrs Hardcastle, both dressed for hunting, at Inverewe, Ross-shire, on 3 October 1906. Mrs Hardcastle's sturdy boots and practical, above-the-ankle skirt show how clothes were adapting to the more vigorous outdoor pursuits in which better-off women were now participating.

A woman in Skye knitting as she walks, perhaps carrying home peat for the fire, about 1905. Many women in rural and fishing communities were expert in doing several things at the same time. Women kept their families supplied with socks, stockings, jerseys and shawls.

May and Effie Graham making music at Bruntsfield Crescent, Edinburgh, 1908. Playing a musical instrument was considered an appropriate accomplishment for young women of middle-class upbringing, although professional participation in the arts was not generally encouraged.

Team of diggers in Shetland, early twentieth century. In crofting communities, women worked on the land when the men were away at the fishing. They are using traditional delving spades to turn the earth. In order to fit into the picture, they are much closer together than they would normally be to work.

'In all the histories, books, papers, articles, accounts and statistics written of Shetland, nothing is more striking than the small account taken of the real inhabitants of Shetland, who alone maintain continuous life in the isles – the women... It is during the spring, summer, and autumn months, while the men are mostly absent that the real work of the crofts is done. The women do it.'
Christina Jamieson, Shetland Times, *22 January 1910*

Gutting and packing herring on the quay at Aberdeen's Fishmarket, 1903. The herring brought in by the boats was gutted and packed in barrels of salt. The women often worked twelve or more hours a day, dealing with 20 to 30 herring a minute, and packing three barrels in an hour. Behind the girls are the baskets used to carry the gutted herring and containers for salt.

'I wouldna go back tae guttin' again, oh no, and I wouldna put nane o' mine tae the guttin'. No. It wis a primitive wey o' workin'. I hated it, I just hated it! In fact to tell you the truth, I wouldna hae gaen tull't, if it wasna fur helpin' the fishin' industry.'
Mrs Evelyn Crockett, Odyssey – The Second Collection, *ed Billy Kay (Edinburgh 1982)*

Bondagers at Cornhill-on-Tweed, Northumberland (just on the English side of the Border), 1908–09. Women who worked on the land in a form of indentured service were known as 'bondagers'. These women are (left to right) B Johnston, L Wastle and K Wastle (sisters). The little girls with grubby faces and pinnies are A Fraser, L Hope, E Fraser and K Hope.

A correspondent writing in *The Countryman* in 1943 described English bondagers:

'Theor wus ony amoont in the north country arl along this side o' the border, by Alnwick and Wooler. They aal wore the seam claes, a black strae bonnet o'er a red hankie, wi' checky bloozes an' a coarse bratty o'er theor flanner skirts. Then they had clootie leggings, tied rund theor legs, an' great beuts. They wore aad stockings o'er theor airms. when they wur stooking corn, to stop the thrustles rippen 'em.'

Although true bondagers, tied to the farm worker who employed them, had disappeared by the mid-nineteenth century, the term was used for female farm workers in the Borders until the Second World War.

Washday, about 1910, Seton parish, East Lothian. One of the most arduous domestic chores was the family wash, invariably carried out by women. The first modern domestic washing machines appeared on the scene in the 1920s, but most households' washing was done by hand until well after the Second World War. At the beginning of the century long skirts and bulkier garments added to the burden. This young woman has eased the strain a little by propping her washtub on on overturned chair. She is wearing a man's bonnet, which gives her a slightly rakish air.

Annual outing of a club (mission) for unmarried mothers, 1908. Providing succour and support to the less privileged was an object of middle-class charitable zeal. This mission was run by Jessie Irvine in Edinburgh's Bread Street. She is the older woman seated at the front, with her daughter, Janetta Agnes Kay, the smartly-dressed young woman to her right. Many of the women here look extremely young, some probably in their mid-teens.

Women, children and ponies at Heisker, North Uist, 1911. Three generations are assembled here, in a natural-looking group that has warmth and charm. The most important member of the group is clearly the older woman in the foreground, in striped skirt and neat black boots.

Pupils of Craigmillar Park College in Edinburgh playing tennis, about 1910. By the end of the previous century it was recognized that fresh air and exercise were as important for girls as for boys. Girls, however, continued to be hampered by long skirts and the view that sporting activity had to be ladylike.

The prospectus for the school offered languages, music, art, dancing, English, History, Geography, Nature Study, Arithmetic, Geometry and Algebra, and emphasized outdoor pursuits:

'Besides Garden Games, Tennis and Net Ball, the College is close to Blackford Hill and Arthur's Seat, where the boarders are taken during the week, as well as for other country walks. They may also enjoy a day's skating, etc. Arrangements may be made for swimming and riding lessons.'

The final year of 1911 at Edinburgh University Medical School, four women among the mass of men. Although women were admitted to study medicine at Edinburgh University in the previous century they were not at first allowed to practise as doctors. By the time this photograph was taken women could pursue the profession for which they were trained, but they remained very much in the minority.

Isabel Emslie entered Edinburgh University medical school at the age of 17 in 1905.

'How any of us had the courage to enter medicine at such a time is a mystery to me. We still studied under a good many disadvantages and observed that the women doctors had to put up with very cavalier treatment by their men colleages, who criticised, patronised or were even blatantly rude to them... The plain dowdy women students were on the whole preferred, for the men could then hoot with laughter and label them all as freaks, jokes or monsters... The men seemed surprised and annoyed that the attractive women could stay the course.'

Isabel Hutton, Memories of a Doctor in War and Peace *(London 1960)*

Suffragettes campaigning in a
Scottish town, much to the interest
of numerous small boys. We do not
know where this is, or who these
women are, but there was strong
support for the suffrage campaign
throughout Scotland.
*Trustees of the National Library of
Scotland*

Addressing an open-air meeting during the campaign for women's suffrage. Women had had little opportunity to gain experience in public life, and it took courage to speak publicly and deal with hecklers and other difficulties.
Trustees of the National Library of Scotland

A bookkeepers' class at Tynecastle Trade School, Edinburgh, about 1914. Offices had begun to recruit women before the end of the nineteenth century, and office work soon became a key occupation for women. The dress of these young women, shirts and ties, reflects a sense that the office conformed to a male image of the business-like, where frills and frivolity would be out of place.

A typewriting class for boys and girls at the Royal High School, Edinburgh, about 1914. The first typewriters were being made in the 1870s and were widespread in offices by the end of the century. From the start they were seen as machines appropriate for women, although there were many male typists also.

Taking a fence, early twentieth century. Many women in the nineteenth century were keen riders, their horsemanship all the more skilled for the fact that they rode sidesaddle. Horse riding was one of the few activities in which women could take part on (almost) the same terms as men.

This ornamental ship is worn to set off a hairstyle created in a Leith Walk, Edinburgh, hairdressing class, part of a 1914 adult education programme. The Edwardian period saw some astonishing hairstyles and headgear. Fruit, flowers and birds were not uncommon, but a ship in full sail must have seemed extreme, even at the time. It is tempting to suggest that as clothes for women became less elaborate and more practical, milliners looked for ways to compensate.

Two girls from Tong, Lewis, employed in a Glasgow munitions factory, 1914–18. Conscription into the forces left an urgent need for women to fill many jobs traditionally held by men. Many rural and working-class women left farm work and domestic service to become 'munitionettes' – women working in munition factories.

THE GREAT WAR

The First World War shattered many conventions and gave scope for women to take on new roles. The most conspicuous of them were the lady tram drivers in Edinburgh and Glasgow, where even the most sceptical of observers had to admit that they were perfectly capable of doing the job.

The photographs depict nurses in the public eye for the first time. They served not only in British hospitals; it was also considered patriotic to serve abroad, and thus – in addition to helping to relieve suffering – there was a chance for travel and new experiences which would never have come the way of a Scottish nurse in the ordinary course of events.

Medical women also came into their own, though the War Office rejected their services. Dr Elsie Inglis of Edinburgh came up with the idea of the Scottish Women's Hospitals for Foreign Service, all-female units of doctors, nurses, orderlies and drivers. The organization was adopted by the Scottish Federation of Women's Suffrage Societies and more than a thousand women went to the battlefronts, achieving great renown.

Working-class women no longer had to remain tied to domestic service. One of the largest munitions factories in the country was at Gretna, and shipbuilders and other firms involved in the war effort were crying out for labour, so girls could now choose to take such a job. It was dangerous work, but they possessed a degree of freedom previously unimaginable. Photographs of them highlighted their role as essential war workers – a role achievable by any woman.

However, attempts to recruit women to work on the land after the men left it for the armed forces proved much harder than in England, because so many Scottish women had been agricultural workers before the war and were now grabbing the chance to get away from the arduous and often lonely outdoor work. Girls flocked to the factories from as far as the Western Isles, but there was less of a culture shock than one might think, as many had previously followed the herring fishing and therefore were used to adapting to different places and environments.

As the war dragged on, women on the Home Front had to contend with increasing shortages of food. Working-class women in particular were disadvantaged by rising prices, but when landlords tried to raise their rents in Glasgow they mounted an astonishingly successful strike, overcoming through their solidarity one form of blatant exploitation.

By the end of the war women over thirty with property qualifications had won the vote and could even stand for Parliament. (Ironically, the first Scottish woman MP, the Duchess of Atholl, had been a leading anti-suffragist before the war.) It has long been said that this was a reward for all the work they did, yet the young women who contributed most to the war effort were still disenfranchized. The true gains of the war were harder to evaluate: the chance of feeling truly useful, of contributing something worthwhile, of showing what women were capable of.

A science class at Portobello Higher Grade School, about 1914. Hands-on science classes for girls were relatively new. Although this science class includes both boys and girls, apparently carrying out the same experiment, it remained difficult for girls to gain entrance to professions in the sciences.

Mothers' class at Towerbank School, Portobello, about 1914. Mothers' classes were run mainly by middle-class women for the less well off. They combined prayer and a religious address with needlework. Later, practical advice on diet, health and childcare was included.

'Sewing allowed the women to sit together without feeling they were neglecting their homes or children, and the clothing they made reconciled husbands to their going. The meetings provided comradeship, the sympathy of other women, rest from arduous labours, and escape from husbands.'
(*C Prochoska, A mother's country: mother's meetings and family welfare in Britain,* History 1989)

Helen Henderson Fairweather, between 1910 and 1920, infants mistress at Ashbank, Monifieth. Miss Fairweather was a teacher for 40 years. Her dignified pose and sophisticated dress ornamented with lace and beads indicate a woman of both elegance and self-confidence. Women teachers and civil servants were forced to resign if they married. Miss Fairweather may have chosen to teach rather than to marry, though equally the fact that she did not marry may have been a consequence of the huge death toll of men in World War One.

The numbers of women teachers continued to increase, without either the status or the pay of the men.

Barbara Gibson was a highly-regarded teacher at Creggans school, near Inveraray, Argyll, photographed in about 1915. The school pre-dated the 1873 Education Act and was supported by the Duke of Argyll. Miss Gibson lost both her arms at the age of nine, in her father's barn threshing mill.

Sister B Henderson, a nurse at Yorkhill War Hospital, Glasgow with Capt Ingham, recovering from having his right leg amputated at the knee, 1918. During the First World War many women, some who had never before considered working, volunteered for hospital work. They dealt with appalling wounds and severe trauma.

Nurses and recovering wounded at a
military hospital, 1914–18.

We do not know where this
photograph was taken, but hospital
provision for the war wounded was
often basic and crowded – as this
picture suggests.

These postwomen from Edzell in Angus took over from the absent men. Women's labour was vital in maintaining essential services in wartime.

AUCHTERMUCHTY PARISH CHURCH
JUNIOR CHOIR—WAR CONCERT, 1915.
"KNITTING SONG"

The Junior Choir of Auchtermuchty Parish Church in Perthshire
contributing to the war effort,
1915. They sang as they knitted:
'We knit for our gallant soldiers
Who fearlessly go to fight

On fields of France and Belgium
For the cause of truth and right.
So long as sounds of strife are heard
And for freedom men are dying,
We'll knit with zest and do our best
To keep the old flag flying.

Our "Muchty" soldier at the front
With pride we all remember.
Such patriotic sons shall force
The Kaiser to surrender.'

MCG

Munitions workers, 1914-18. Many factories had to convert from peace-time to wartime production, and to recruit women as their workforce. The uniform worn by these women developed in response to the need for practical and safe clothing. During the First World War many women got used to wearing trousers, but those who worked in the public eye – on the trams or as postwomen, for example – usually wore skirts.

A laundry class at a Tynecastle Trade School, Edinburgh, about 1914. Tynecastle offered training in a number of trades for boys and girls. At either side the girls are learning to use flat irons, while at the back they are handwashing, using big blocks of soap. Vocational training in areas such as cookery, laundry, bookkeeping, dressmaking and millinery provided useful skills, but views on what was considered acceptable work for girls were limited by class as well as gender.

Jane Patrick, photographed in 1918, was secretary of the Glasgow Anarchists and in 1921 of the Glasgow Central Branch of the Anti-parliamentary Communist Federation. The First World War left a legacy of radicalism in which women participated, although men were dominant. Jane Patrick later worked in Madrid with the Republican Government, 1936-7.

BETWEEN THE WARS

With thousands of demobilized men arriving back in Scotland it was inevitable that many women lost their jobs. And, when the brief post-war boom was followed by a severe Depression, ex-servicemen demanded to be given jobs in place of the women who had held them during the war.

Not all women workers fared alike. The Sex Disqualification (Removal) Act of 1919 opened the law and other professions to women, but those who worked in the civil service during the war years, envisaging fine career prospects, found themselves confined to the lower echelons of the service. And the women who had been urged to train as doctors discovered the doors of the teaching hospitals once again closed in their faces. Women teachers were not granted equal pay, but on their salary they could live a more comfortable life than a married man with a family, so the teaching profession remained the preserve of women, at least in its lower grades. A woman had to resign from most jobs if she got married.

The war had put a stop to the Scottish fishing industry, but now it resumed, and once again the teams of female packers and gutters were in demand. They were guaranteed a minimum wage, however bad the season, and had the hope of a good one with a spending spree at the end of it, so this was a godsend to poor families.

The Land Settlement (Scotland) Act of 1919 created some 6000 crofts and small-holdings for ex-servicemen and their families. No smallholding could survive without the wife and children working as hard, if not harder, than the holder. Mechanization was slow in coming, especially to smaller farms, and traditional ways of working continued in this period. This way of life offered scant financial reward, though the holding could be passed on to one's children. Photographers were drawn to the sight of women working on the land.

After the freedom of wartime employment, women had little desire to return to domestic service, though as the job market continued to shrink many had no choice. By 1931 some 7% of the total female population in Scotland were employed as domestic servants, similar to the percentage in 1911. However, as male unemployment accelerated in the 1930s, more women became (as they had long been in Dundee) the breadwinners of the family. Many of the new industries – artificial fibres, plastic, electrical products etc – required adaptability but no particular skill or brawn, and women, who could be paid less, were therefore preferred. Openings for women clerical workers also continued to grow: in 1911 there were 33,570 of them in Scotland; by 1911 they numbered 173,370. But no one was interested in photographing them.

During the 1920s hemlines went up, stays went out, and dresses allowed maximum freedom of movement. Young women, it seemed, were emancipated at last – but not for long. In the thirties hems went down, corsets returned, and marriage, motherhood and housework were again the ideals to which women were suppose to aspire. The first domestic appliances were on the market, but they could be afforded only by the wealthy, and it could still plausibly be claimed that running a home was a full-time occupation. Women workers, who were expected to feed and look after the family when they got home, would have laughed at the thought.

Photography was no longer the preserve of the professional standing behind a rigid camera. It was something nearly everyone could afford to indulge in, so the range of subjects widened.

The wedding of Christina Macrae and Alex Mathieson, a farmer of Tighnahiuch and Duncournie, Fernitosh, Ross-shire, 1919. They are, from left to right, Daisy Mackenzie, teacher; Murdo Mackenzie, Minister from Thurso; Alex Mathieson; Christina Macrae; her brother, Murdo Macrae and mother, Mrs Macrae.

Beatrice Grace Dickson (born 1900) drawing water from the public well in the Wynd, Gifford, East Lothian, for her mother who did the washing for the men in the bothy at Yester House, about 1920. In many respects, the Great War and its end made little difference to rural life. In town and country fetching the daily supply of water was not uncommon, as many homes were without water.

The Sinclair family of Boat's House, Symbister, Whalsay, Shetland. At the back, from the left: Spark, the dog, Sandy Jardine, Chrissie Sinclair, Robbie Sinclair, Davie Sinclair. Centre: Laura Sinclair. Front, from the left: Ennie Sinclair, Mrs R Sinclair, Sandy Sinclair, Ellie Sinclair, Willie Sinclair.
J D Rattar

'La Mia Rosettes', a novelty dancing and singing act, probably performing in Glasgow, 1920s. These girls epitomize the radical changes that followed the First World War. Short skirts and bobbed hair suggest a breaking away from restraint and convention. Jazz and the Charleston arrived and dancing became a favourite pastime, to take part in and to watch.

Peigi MacRae milking Dora at the door of her cottage, North Glendale, South Lochboisdale, South Uist, 1930-1. It is obviously a breezy day. The cow's back legs have been tied together with a *buarach* to keep it from kicking the pail. Care of the dairy cattle, milking and the making of butter and cheese was traditionally in the hands of women.
Margaret Fay Shaw Campbell

Fisher girls, C McIntosh and Martha Fraser, spangled with fish scales, at work gutting herring, Nairn, 1920s. The slight blurring of the hands suggest the speed at which they worked – three barrels packed in an hour, with 800 to 1000 herrings each.

Mrs Sandison at her spinning wheel, Balta Sound, Unst, Shetland, 1926. Domestic spinning continued in parts of the Hebrides and Northern Isles until well after the Second World War. Although the dress is twentieth century, this picture could have been taken a hundred years earlier. The custom continued of sitting outside at the spinning wheel, making the most of the light.

Mrs Gillies, one of the last St Kildans, seated in front of her house. This photograph was taken the day before St Kilda was evacuated, in August 1930. She calmly continued to knit, using wool plucked from the local Soay sheep and spun at home. Most of her own clothes would have been dyed and woven or knitted on the island.
Alasdair Alpin Macgregor

Nurses Stronach, Cameron, Melville and Cameron, with their small charges, North Uist, Inverness-shire, 1926.

A cottage interior, Smerclate, South Uist, Inverness-shire, 1934. As in the photograph of Mrs Sandison, only the woman's dress indicates that this picture was taken in the twentieth century.

By 1934 this traditional blackhouse with an open fire and hard-packed earth floor would have been rare, even in the remoter islands. The smoke from the fire made its way out through the thatch. The dog and two cats are making the most of the hot cinders. The furniture could be homemade, possibly from driftwood. The display of crockery indicates a pride in the interior, whatever the lack of 'modern' equipment.

Women wearing traditional 'uglies' (bonnets which protected from the sun and wind) working on the bulb farm of Walter Blom and Son at Westbarns, Dunbar, East Lothian. The picture was probably taken in 1936, the year the farm was started up, with the help of expertise from Holland.

Angela Varecchi, with her travelling barrel organ. Mrs Varecchi lived in Edinburgh's Grassmarket during the winter. In the summer she travelled round Scotland with a cage of love birds, a monkey (riding on the pony), and two dogs.

Mairi Campbell (Bean Aonghuis Ruaidh) collecting seaweed, South Uist, Inverness-shire, in the 1920s. Seaweed was a traditional source of fertilizer, used on lazybeds for growing potatoes. In parts of the west of Scotland close to the shore seaweed is still used as a fertilizer. *Margaret Fay Shaw Campbell*

Shearing sheep at Points Sheiling, near Stornoway, Lewis, 1936. Shepherding and sheep-shearing were more normally male occupations, but when required women took part. The heavy casualties of the First World War and the attractions of work in Scotland's central belt deprived many families of their menfolk.

Mary Morrison doing the washing at Crudie, near Turriff, Aberdeenshire, 1930s. The wooden tub of an earlier period has been replaced by zinc, but that makes no difference to the nature of the job. The over-turned chair is utilized, as it had been decades before.

Mrs Mary Mowat and her daughter
Sheila boating at Dunbar, East
Lothian, about 1926. The seaside
towns within easy reach of
Edinburgh were well-established for
holidays and day trips.

Off on an outing from Portmahomack, Ross-shire, in a charabanc motor bus – the first bus in the area, 1930s. The bus was owned by Dan Mackay, who ran a garage in nearby Tain. This may be a Women's Guild or SWRI group. The basket attached to the footplate suggests that a picnic is in the offing.

Miss Pitcaithly curling on the Moncreiffe Curling Club's pond at Bridge of Earn, Perthshire, 1937. In 1899 women took part in the Scottish bonspiel, at Carsebeck, for the first time. The men were nervous at the prospect of being beaten by a team of women, but their fears were not realized. As the twentieth century progressed women participated more widely in outdoor sports and activities. Miss Pitcaithly is about to slide the curling stone along the ice, and will use the brush to smooth its passage. *Star Photos*

Staff of J W Mackie Bros on an outing, 1930s. Third and fourth from the left are Grace McLeod and Janet Murray. Annual staff outings became popular between the wars. Improvements in transport and conditions of employment brought day trips and holidays within the means of a growing number of people.

On Gullane beach, East Lothian: Mrs Greta Young, her son Charles and Mrs Frances Wilson, 1937-8. The two women had been at Dalry Primary School in Edinburgh together, and met up again through their husbands, members of the same Masonic Lodge. Greta was a short-hand typist for seven years before she married and Frances a hairdresser in a West End salon for eleven years. Charles, in the picture, was the Youngs' only son. The Wilsons had a daughter. The two families often went out together in the Youngs' Hillman.
Frank Wilson

Holidaymakers on their way down the Clyde to Rothesay, 1930s. The 1930s were the heyday of Rothesay as a day trip destination. Outings like this provided a welcome break from the relentless responsibilities of home and work. The man bent over his box camera is a reminder that photography was becoming a pastime which increasing numbers could afford.

The original caption lists the names as follows: Robert Anderson, Andrew Marshall, Mrs Sutherland, Peter Kinghorn, George Sutherland, Mrs Marshall. The women's identities are masked by their married status.

Kilchattan Scottish Women's Rural Institute (SWRI), Bute, 1920s. The range of expressive faces under cloche hats suggests a group of determined but good-humoured women.

They are, back row from left: Mrs Gilmour, Mrs McAlister, Miss Nellie Bell, Mrs Begg, Mrs Little, Mrs Massey or Massie, Mrs Stewart, Mrs McFarlane. Middle row: – Martin, Nessie Logan, Anne Gilmour, Agnes Mathewson, Mrs McArthur, Euphie Galbraith, Miss Jean Baillie, Miss Lizzie McFie. Front row: Jean Speirs, Hettie Steel, Janet Gilmour, Agnes Murray, Margaret Crawford, Miss Marian Morrison, Jean McMillan.

The SWRI was formed in 1917 to provide support and education in rural areas. Its founder was Catherine Blair, née Shields, a suffragette and wife of an East Lothian farmer. She also set up the Mak' Merry pottery.

Holiday makers at the Dhu Rock, West Port, Dunbar, by the swimming pool, 1936. A fine range of swimwear is displayed – a similar style for men and women. Two decades earlier, to have revealed so much flesh in mixed company would have been unthinkable.
G N Day

Brushmaking for the firm of James Dawson in Dalkeith, Midlothian, 1937. The woman here is polishing up the handles of finished brushes.

Jenny Forgie had been a maid in a minister's house before she became postwoman in Luss, Argyll. This photograph was taken in the 1930s. She covered a wide area, which included Luss Glen, a two-mile stretch, uphill most of the way. She cycled, with the mailbag strapped to the handlebars. She did the run to Edentaggart at the head of the glen every day, and twice a week went as far as Glenmacairn along a very rough track.

Rag picker sorting her collection of rags, Edinburgh, about 1934. At a time when recycling was customary, rag pickers were a common sight on town streets. Some encouraged children to chase up their parents for rags by offering balloons in exchange, while others traded crockery. This woman is sorting and grading rags, probably destined for the quality paper-making industry.

Making tea in a Ballachulish home in the 1930s. The kettle has boiled on the hearth. To the right is a box bed. The domestic environment is much the same as it would have been before 1914. For the women responsible for maintaining homes such as these, the twentieth century had not, by the '30s, brought significant change.

Soup kitchen at the Vale of Leven Communist Party premises in Alexandria, Dunbartonshire, 1930s. The soup kitchen was organized by George Halkett (in the rear, wearing a cap) with the help of local woman who cooked, served and washed up. Local shopkeepers donated bones, vegetables, bread, tea and sugar.

The wedding of Maggie Mennie, housemaid, to a farmer, Methlick, Aberdeenshire, 1926. Her sister is the bridesmaid. The young women wear fashionable dresses and hairstyles. The wedding outfits of both men and women were very different from their working wear, on which fashion would have little influence.

Edinburgh Ladies Cycling Club in Lower Lanark Road, Edinburgh, 1930s. The Club met every Sunday morning in Waterloo Place, Edinburgh, and set off to their chosen destination. From left to right, they are Nellie Burt, Jean Webster, May Sloan, Nan Leslie, Nan Knowles, Peggy Forsyth and Gladys Williamson.

Women workers with horses on a Lothian farm, World War Two. This picture featured in *The Scotsman* calendar for 1943. The women are about to start off on their day's work. In wartime the contribution of women to maintaining the productivity of farms was vital. They may have been members of the Women's Land Army, who would normally have worn uniform only on formal occasions.

THE SECOND WORLD WAR

By the outbreak of the Second World War unmarried women supported themselves as a matter of course, and nine girls out of ten worked from the time they left school until they got married. But the scope of the work, and the chances for married women, were transformed during the war years.

As the photographs show, the sight of women in uniform became common in Scotland at that time. Conscription of women – with the choice of service in the forces or full-time work in essential industries or on the land – was new to this war. Girls of eighteen and married women were not officially conscripted but came under the direction of the Minister of Labour; in practice the distinction made little difference since the order had to be obeyed.

The war meant that once again jobs considered 'unfeminine' in peacetime were re-evaluated, and women who enjoyed driving, say, or engineering, had the opportunity of following their bent. And nurses again emerged into the limelight. The idea that running a home kept a woman fully occupied – proclaimed so assiduously in the inter-war years – was discredited, and most married women had no choice *but* to go out to work.

City women were recruited to work on the land, even – as the photographs show – in such physically demanding occupations as forestry. Meanwhile, wives and daughters kept farms, crofts and smallholdings going in the absence of their menfolk, as they had always done. Prisoners of war sometimes helped, and the contact with men of other nationalities, whether Italian prisoners or American soldiers, was another new feature for Scottish women. Some marriages did not survive the social dislocation and the new sexual freedom.

It was a war in which civilians suffered greatly, especially in cities. No longer was 'home' a place of safety which a serviceman would think of without fear for his family. Air raids on Scottish cities, for example the particularly drastic bombing of Clydebank, were endured by women and children. Rationing of food and clothing were less dramatic, but more constant, miseries. The opportunities to escape the home environment and be valued for a worthwhile contribution to the war effort were overshadowed – far more than in the First World War – by what had to be endured on the Home Front. Yet many Scottish women remember the war as the high point in their lives.

A fête to raise money for the Linthill Red Cross, Lilliesleaf, Roxburghshire, summer 1940. Women were the stalwarts of such money-raising activities, organizing them, making, baking and collecting, and staffing the stalls. Pictured from the left, Agnes and Nanny Brown, daughters of the local baker, and Jean Robinson. A pageant was performed at the fête, and Agnes and Nanny are still wearing their costumes.

On that afternoon news was coming through about the return of troops rescued from Dunkirk. When the 6 o'clock news announced that all those who could had returned, Jean Robinson broke down – she had heard nothing from her husband Jim. But the good news came a few days later that Jim was safe.

Sphagnum moss being made into dressings by volunteers at an Edinburgh depot. Sphagnum was highly absorbent, and there was a long tradition of using it for wound dressings. A striking feature of this photograph is that almost all the women are wearing hats.

Jean C Matthew (with glasses) of the Voluntary Aid Detachment (VAD) showing the Duchess of Gloucester around a bandage and dressing depot in Edinburgh, 1939-45.

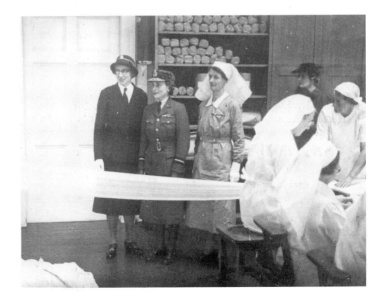

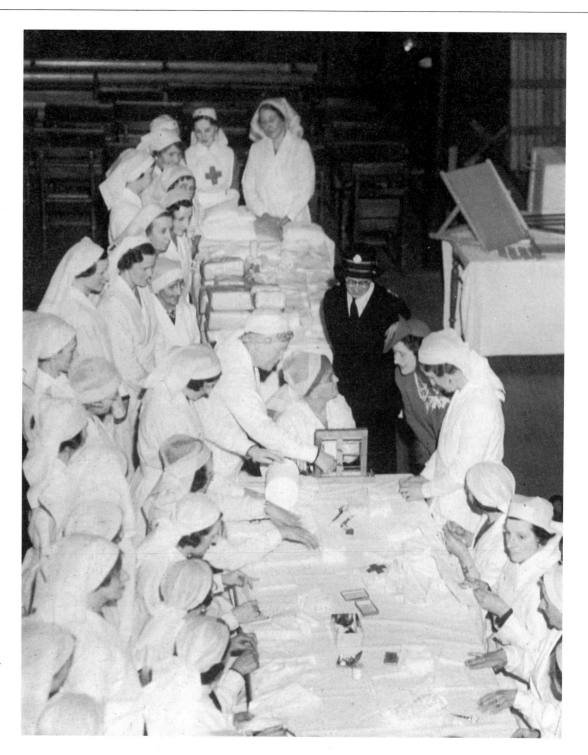

Jean Matthew again, this time showing the Queen, now the Queen Mother, around a Hospital Supplies Depot run by the VAD in Edinburgh, 1939-45.

Laying in with the axe. A Women's Timber Corps member cutting a wedge-shape into one side of a tree to ensure that it will fall naturally in that direction when sawn on the other side. This was probably taken in Angus, about 1942.

The Women's Timber Corps was set up in 1942 to help maintain the vital supply of timber. The work was very hard, resulting in blistered, bleeding hands from tree-felling, as well as aching muscles. Many of the women were completely unused to hard physical labour.

Dinner-time in the woods. Members of the Women's Timber Corps having a break, 1942–45. The usual working day was 8–12 noon and 12.30 to 5pm.

A man commented, 'Mostly they lived a primitive life in bothies or cottages or, where woods lay in isolated parts, in the lofts of stables. Sanitation was non-existent, and for bathing they used a galvanised zinc bath which had to be filled with hot water by kettle. It was a hard, tough, dirty life but I cannot recall one murmur of complaint...'

Two members of the Women's Timber Corps sharpening an axe blade on a grindstone, probably also at one of the Angus camps, about 1942. It is likely this photograph dates from the early days of the WTC, as the women are wearing the uniform of the Women's Forestry Service, which preceded the Timber Corps.

'Driving Mars – my war horse.' Jean Comrie driving a tractor at Drummie, Foulis Wester, Perthshire, in 1944. Women driving tractors were a common sight in wartime. Before and after, their participation in the increasing mechanization of agriculture was very limited.
The photograph was taken at potato lifting – the implement in the background is a potato digger. Like many farmers' daughters, Jean Comrie was designated in a reserved occupation, and was involved in all aspects of farm life.

The wedding of Lilian and George Allan, at Halkirk, Caithness, in the 1940s. George had lost both his legs. On the right is Thelma Allan, George's sister, and seated are Lilian's parents.

Women of the Women's Royal Naval Service, HMS *Jackdaw*, being trained in the use of a Lewis anti-aircraft gun. HMS *Jackdaw* was a Royal Naval Air Station from about 1940 to 1947, with planes flying on patrol across the North Sea as far as Norway.

Mrs Morrison spinning, Rodel,
Harris, 1939.

A fish wife from Newhaven, selling shellfish in an Edinburgh street in the 1940s. Still dressed in the traditional striped apron, this woman could have been transplanted from the previous century, when fish wives were a common sight on Edinburgh's streets. The size of the creel suggests the weight that she carried.

Making butter, Ness, Lewis, probably 1940s. Helping their mothers with domestic tasks has always been a major influence on girls' choice of occupation when adult. Much of the affect of wartime on women's opportunities was temporary.

Ishbel Taylor, a porter and relief crossing keeper at Killearn and Dumgoyne stations on the Blane Valley line from early 1943 to 1951. As well as agricultural produce and livestock, during the war aviation fuel and ammunition, locally stored, came through the stations. Long nights were spent in the blacked-out Dumgoyne station, waiting to open the gates for the huge double-headed trains with their dangerous loads.

These women were carriage cleaners on the LNER (London and North East Railway). They were photographed at Bridgton Cross station, Glasgow, in 1946. They are, back, from the left: Peggy Currie, Annie Tarleton, Meg Douglas, Bella Logue. Front: Maggie Macarthur, Kate Duffy, Annie Montgomery, Helen Maitland (in mourning for her husband who died during the D-Day landings), Nancy Pickering, Frances Walker.

Peggy Currie went back to work after her husband was killed in a road accident in 1942. Helen Maitland's husband was in the army. Annie Tarleton and Bella Logue were both widows. Meg Douglas had an elderly invalid husband. The others were unmarried, and had probably been directed to work for the railways.

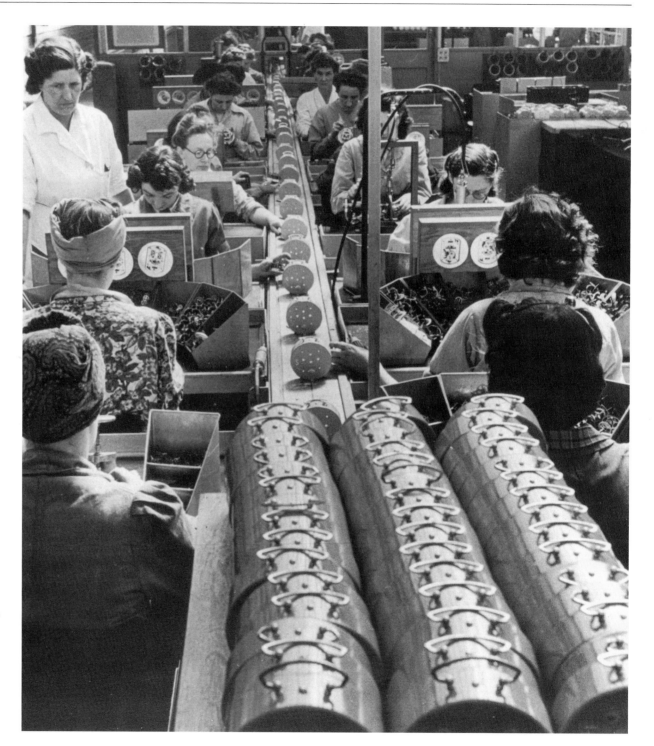

The assembly line of a clock factory, UK Time Co of Dundee, 1940s or '50s. The war drew many women into the factories, and they continued to be mainstays of some aspects of assembly line work, especially as their labour was often cheaper than men's.

AFTER THE WAR WAS OVER

At the end of the war women were not elbowed out of their jobs as brusquely as in 1918-20. That was partly because many married women did not wait to be asked but left of their own accord, especially after the special arrangements (like nurseries) made to attract them were withdrawn. Looking after home and family was yet again touted as the most desirable occupation for a woman. As a reaction against overalls and uniforms, clothing became more elaborate and restricting, with corsets and padding and long skirts, signalling the importance of looking 'womanly' and attractive to the opposite sex.

The last few years of the 1950s were boom years. Many more jobs became available, and since there was already full employment, married women were again in urgent demand. The 18% of British married women working in 1947 went up to 33% in 1957, and by 1961 more than half of all those in paid employment were married women. In a double-income household men still paid for the basics, but all kinds of extras – labour-saving devices, holidays, a car – now became affordable. Domestic appliances transformed housework, and the servant class all but disappeared.

Nursing and teaching were still the most popular careers for women, with improved conditions in both since demand exceeded supply. The teaching profession finally accepted the principle of equal pay in 1955, and it was fully implemented in 1961.

To identify a photograph of a Scottish woman working on the land as belonging to the 1950s, rather than the 1920s, 30s or 40s, one usually has to rely on clothing, for her traditional work changed little. Heavy farm work, such as ploughing and harvesting, had long since changed, but only with the advent of the milking machine and the battery hen system in the late 1950s and early 60s did women's role on the land make a radical break with the past.

After the 1950s, when there was a great emphasis on luring the opposite sex, the 1960s saw the explosion of 'women's lib'. Limiting fertility was now within a woman's control. Young women had spending power unimagined by earlier generations, and with role models such as Lulu they could even aspire to pop stardom. The mini-skirt and hot pants were the fashion for the young, and opportunities for spending leisure time enjoyably, whether eating out, going to the cinema or to dances, or taking part in sports, had never been greater.

The pendulum of liberalism/repression, of fashion, of attitudes, of women as sub-ordinate or equal to men, will no doubt continue to swing, and one generation will inevitably see a younger turn their backs on hard-won gains. But for every two steps forward there is surely no more than one back. For who, before this time, ever thought of looking at a volume of photographs of Scottish women? – neither drudges nor fantasy figures but partners in every aspect of life.

Gathering the shaws, the parts of the
potato plants above ground, before
the passage of the potato digger.
This photograph was taken at the
Scottish Institute of Agriculture farm
at Howden House, Mid Calder,
Midlothian, about 1950.

Margaret Mackenzie serving in Mrs
Waters's shop in Braemore Road,
Dunbeath, Caithness, 1940s or '50s.
Shops large and small were a major
source of employment for women.
A range of typical foodstuffs is in
evidence – tinned soup and beans,
processed cheese, corned beef. It
took at least a decade to leave
wartime scarcity behind, and the
rationing of some foods continued
until 1954.

Milking at Mairead a Bhodaich, Lewis, about the 1940s. In many areas of Scotland, the roles of women were hardly affected by either war or technology.

Mrs Carnegie working at A W Buchan and Co, a Portobello pottery, about 1948. She is spraying earthenware 'pigs' with glazing solution before they were placed in the kiln for firing. The Portobello pottery industry dated back to the 1760s. Buchans was the longest lived, closing in 1972.

Operating the jolly in a pottery, probably A W Buchan and Co in Portobello, 1948. 'Jollying' is a way of making pottery through a combination of throwing on a wheel and casting on moulds. The clay is thrown into a revolving mould and fashioned by machine. The economic gains of factory work were balanced by the physical demands – long shifts, dirty conditions and being on the feet all day.

Machine weaving at Buccleuch Mills, Langholm, Dumfriesshire, about 1950. The photographer noted:

'Power loom: attended by alert girls, each operating 2 machines. Amid a deafening clatter of flying shuttles they watch the weft thread from the swift moving shuttles weaving the warp. So Scotch tweeds in their attractive patterns and colouring "grow" at an an amazing speed.'
David Innes

Women working at the Newton
Carpet Works, Newton-on-Ayr,
1950s.
David Innes

Behind the scenes at an Eriskay
wedding, Inverness-shire, about
1961. Refreshments for a large number of guests are being prepared in
an improvised kitchen. Although
working hard (and dressed in everyday clothes) the women give every
impression of enjoying themselves.
K Robertson

The wedding reception of the Marquis of Douglas and Clydesdale and Lady Elizabeth Percy, held at the Assembly Rooms in Edinburgh, probably the 1950s. They were married in St Giles Cathedral.
Scottish Pictorial

Veteran suffragettes. From the left, Helen Crawfurd, Miss I H Whelland, Hilda M Monaghan (Chairwoman of Women for Westminster, Glasgow Branch), Helen Tainsk, Janet Barrowman, and seated, Mrs Billington-Greig.

The photograph may have been taken in 1952, at the fiftieth anniversary of the Glasgow and West of Scotland Association for Women's Suffrage, or in 1953, the fiftieth anniversary of the Women's Social and Political Union.

At the Trinity Fair, Brechin, Angus, 1957. A fairground family preparing their evening meal before the evening's work. The steaming pot is slung from a tripod over a wood fire. Travelling fairs remain a feature of Scottish life.
P K McLaren

Ethel Moyes with her granddaughter Doreen, 1956. Every Easter Doreen and her family came from Glasgow to stay with her grandmother in Marchmont Street, Edinburgh. The photograph was taken by Doreen's father, a press photographer. Doreen grew up to become a photographer herself and is now on the staff of the National Museums of Scotland.
Harry Moyes

Festival landlady, Edinburgh, 1958. Mrs Dunne-Maher provided accommodation for performers during the Edinburgh International Festival. Over the years she acquired a collection of photographs and souvenirs from her guests, some of which are seen here. The Edinburgh Festival, since its beginnings in 1947, has provided seasonal employment for large numbers of women, in staffing hotels, guest houses and performance venues.
Photo Illustrations

Fish packing, Aberdeen, 1958. These extra-large kippers are being packed for the American market. The fish processing industry remained dependent on female labour, as it had been a century earlier.
Coopey of Aberdeen

Postwoman Joan Niven using the private bucket bridge over the River Findhorn on the Cawdor Estate, Nairn, 1960. The 'bucket,' operated by a pulley system, carried passengers across the river.
J Topham Ltd

Caravan washday, 1950s or '60s. The use of the traditional tub and washboard did not disappear with readier access to washing machines. The basic tasks of keeping clean remained hard labour for some, and labour that continued to be carried out mainly by women.
P K McLaren

At work in the laboratory of the Kirkcudbright Creamery, Kirkcudbrightshire, in the 1950s. The milk coming into the creamery and the powder being produced have to be constantly checked. Food processing was a growing industry, offering employment opportunities and affecting women's lives in the kitchen.
David Innes

Mrs John Hutchison 'rooing' sheep, at Newtown, Brae, Shetland in 1962. Shetland sheep shed their fleece in the summer. The traditional way of removing loose wool is by 'rooing', or plucking. Today, most Shetland sheep are clipped.

Pumping water into an enamel bucket, the smithy, Badenscoth, Aberdeenshire, 1975.
Alexander Fenton NMS

Haymaking at North Tolsta, Lewis, Ross-shire, in the 1960s. This young woman is clearly having a good time, but does not look as if she is dressed for serious farm work.

On the ice on Loch Leven, February 1959. The occasion is a curling match, but an ice skating pram-pusher must nevertheless have been an unusual sight. Both the pram and the woman's outfit, tartan trews and duffle jacket, are typical late fifties style.
P K McLaren and British Transport Commission

Skiers Nancy Girvan (left) and her sister Hannah taking a break for refreshment, mid-1950s. The sisters were proprietors of Inverarnain Hotel in Glen Falloch at the head of Loch Lomond. The hotel was used by mountaineers and skiers, and Nancy and Hannah sometimes joined their guests. At that time there were no chair-lifts or tows and skiing was mainly cross-country. On this occasion, the trip got no further than Killin golf course, Perthshire, as the roads beyond were impassable.
T Weir

Baking bannocks on a traditional girdle, suspended on a swey over the fire, at Turnabrain, Angus, in 1967. More bannocks are toasting around the edge of the grate. The baker is using a bannock spade to turn them. Bannocks, made from barley or oatmeal, fat and water, have been a long-established feature of the Scots diet.

'A singer sweet and heroic': Jeannie Robertson, folk singer, with some of her records, photographed in 1963. Jeannie Robertson, who died in 1975, was a key figure in the folk revival of the 1950s and '60s. From an Aberdeenshire travelling family, her renditions of traditional ballads, many nearly forgotten, were particularly powerful.
Coopey of Aberdeen

The singer Lulu performing in Glasgow at the outset of her solo career, 1965. Lulu was part of the rock music explosion of the 1960s, which changed the face and the sound of popular music.

Jean Richardson, aged 95, boiling a kettle on her kitchen range, at her home in Newhaven, Edinburgh, 1967. Even in the 1960s kitchen interiors and equipment varied enormously. Mrs Richardson's domestic chores had probably changed little over the 55 years she had lived here.

Preparing dinner for the sheep shearers, Glenesk, Angus, 1968. Another example of an improvised kitchen (although there is a refrigerator), this time in what looks like a barn, with a rake and hay net hanging up on the left. Many country women were adept at feeding large numbers in difficult circumstances.
Alexander Fenton NMS

An SWRI class on 'collage' embroidery (appliqué), Carberry Tower, Inveresk, Midlothian, 1967.
Scotland's Magazine Collection

Women – and a man – demonstrating for equal pay, probably at the Scottish Trade Unions Conference, 1967. 'Barbara' may be Barbara Castle, then Secretary of State for Employment. The man is W McQuilton, and the women third from the right is Agnes Maclean.
Ian MacDougall

In Clark's bakery, Annfield Street, Dundee, 1973. Going for the messages – domestic shopping – has traditionally been one of the house-wife's tasks. This father and son family business was closing and moving to a new housing scheme at Charleston.

Shopping for food now more likely means a visit to the supermar-ket, sometimes as a family outing, but the main responsibility for buy-ing food still lies with women.

Gala Day at Ratho, Midlothian, 1972. On the cusp of fashion: the mini-skirt still flourishes, but hems have also plunged to the ankle. The hint of a flared trouser leg is also vis-ible. Mini-skirts and flared trousers would soon disappear, to make a reappearance in the 1990s.
Gavin Sprott

Perth 'hingie', 1973. The tenement
window traditionally provided a
view of street life and a means of
relating to the community.
Alexander Fenton NMS

Mrs Watson, in her nineties, Crail, Fife, 1970s. Clearly still vigorous, Mrs Watson is pegging out a Crail football team shirt. She laundered the football gear for the local club for many years. Eventually, the club presented her with a washing machine which greatly insulted her – she thought this was a hint that she wasn't doing the work well enough.

Mairi Robinson, editor-in-chief of the *Concise Scots Dictionary*, published by Aberdeen University Press and the Scottish National Dictionary Association in 1985. She is seen at work in the Association's offices in Edinburgh University's School of Scottish Studies, George Square, Edinburgh, in 1985.
Doreen Moyes, NMS

Sitting by the window of a house in
the Hebrides, 1960s. The woman is
knitting, the cat is enjoying the
sunshine. This photograph could
have been taken at any time in the
last hundred years.

BIBLIOGRAPHY

ADAM, Ruth. *A Woman's Place 1910-1975*. New York, 1975.

BARNES, Ishbel. 'Janet Kennedy' (unpublished paper).

BUCHAN, Margaret. The Social Organization of Fisher Girls In Glasgow. Women's Studies Group. *Uncharted Lives*. Glasgow, 1983.

CHEAPE, Hugh. The Role of Women in Traditional Celtic Society in Scotland. *Journal of Agricultural Museums*. Budapest, 1987.

DEVINE, T M. Women Workers, 1850-1914. In Devine, T M (ed) *Farm Servants and Labour in Lowland Scotland 1770-1914*. Edinburgh, 1984.

DORIAN, Nancy. *The Tyranny of Tide*. Ann Arbor, 1985.

GORDON, Eleanor. Women's Sphere. In Fraser, W Hamish and Morris, R J (eds) *People and Society in Scotland*, Vol 2. Edinburgh, 1990.

HOUSTON, R A. Women in the Economy and Society of Scotland, 1500-1800, in Houston, R A and Whyte, I D (eds) *Scottish Society 1500-1800*. Cambridge, 1989.

MARSHALL, Rosalind. *Virgins and Viragos*. London, 1983.

MARWICK, Arthur. *Women at War*. London, 1977.

MITCHISON, Rosalind and LENEMAN, Leah. *Sexuality and Social Control – Scotland 1660-1780*. Oxford, 1989.

ROBERTS, Elizabeth. *Women's Work 1840-1940*. Basingstoke, 1988.

RUBINSTEIN, David. *Before the Suffragettes: Women's Emancipation in the 1890s*. Basingstoke, 1986.

ACKNOWLEDGEMENTS

Auchindrain Museum
Biggar Museum Trust
Tom Breheny
Charles J Burnett Esq, Ross Herald
Jean Comrie
Crail Museum
Rosemary A Crawford
Robert Currie, Strathaven
W G Dey, FRIBA
Mrs Mary B Drain (daughter of George Halkett)
Dunbeath Preservation Trust
Ian J Fleming
Gallacher Memorial Library, STUC, Glasgow
Glencoe and North Lorn Folk Museum
Glenesk Folk Museum
Göteborgs Historiska Museum
A G Ingram Ltd, Photographers
Thomas L Jenkins
Kilchattan Bay SWRI, Kilchattan Bay, Isle of Bute
Knock School Centenary Collection 1878, Isle of Lewis
John Lawson, Nairn
Lothian Region Social Work Department
Bonny Macadam
Rachel M Macdonald, Stornoway (Angus M Macdonald Collection of photographs)
Ian MacDougall, Scottish Labour History Society
MacGrory Collection, Argyll and Bute District Library
Mrs Isabel McKay
Mrs Margaret Mackenzie (Dunbeath Preservation Trust)
Gus Maclean
Doreen Moyes, National Museums of Scotland

Nairn Fishertown Museum
Ness Historical Trust, Isle of Lewis
Mrs Sheila Pannell
Mrs Beatrice Grace Paterson, née Dickson
Mrs Jean N D Robinson
Roxburgh District Museums (Hawick Museum)
Mrs Joyce M Sanderson (Dr C W Graham's Collection)
Scottish Photography Archive (Riddell Collection)
Margaret Fay Shaw
Shetland Museum
Jean G Stirling
Tain and District Museum
Tong Historical Project
Tom Weir
Louise Wilson, daughter of the photographer Frank Wilson

Special thanks are also due to the late Jim J Wilson of Roslin who, with his wife Nell, discovered, preserved and researched the Steuart family's collection of photographs. An account of their work can be read in *The Steuarts of Mount Esk. In Focus 1887-1900*, copies of which can be found in Roslin Library and the Ethnological Archive; and also in 'The Steuarts of Mount Esk: a Photographic legacy', *Scottish Local History* 20, February 1990, Scottish Local History Forum, 5-7.

The picture selection and writing of captions would not have been possible without the extensive help and interest of Dorothy Kidd, Curator of the Scottish Ethnological Archive. Thanks also to Naomi Tarrant, NMS Curator of Costume.

COUNTIES

1 Shetland Islands
2 Orkney Islands
3 Caithness
4 Sutherland
5 Ross & Cromarty
6 Inverness-shire
7 Nairn
8 Moray
9 Banffshire
10 Aberdeenshire
11 Kincardineshire
12 Angus
13 Perthshire
14 Argyll
15 Bute
16 Fife
17 Kinross-shire
18 Clackmannanshire
19 Stirlingshire
20 Dunbartonshire
21 West Lothian
22 Midlothian
23 East Lothian
24 Berwickshire
25 Roxburghshire
26 Selkirkshire
27 Peeblesshire
28 Lanarkshire
29 Ayrshire
30 Renfrewshire
31 Wigtownshire
32 Kirkcudbrightshire
33 Dumfriesshire

SCALE OF MILES

0   20   40   60   80

N